ETHICAL DEBATES

Birth Control

JACQUI BAILEY

WAYLAND

First published in 2009
by Wayland

Copyright © Wayland 2009

Wayland
338 Euston Road
London NW1 3BH

Wayland Australia
Level 17/207 Kent Street
Sydney NSW 2000

Commissioning editor: Jennifer Sanderson
Designer: Rita Storey
Picture researcher: Kathy Lockley
Proofreader: Susie Brooks

British Library Cataloguing in
Publication Data
  Bailey, Jacqui
  Birth control. - (Ethical debates)
  1. Birth control - Moral and ethical
  aspects - Juvenile literature
  I. Title
  176

ISBN: 978 07502 5657 5

Printed in China

Wayland is a division of
Hachette Children's Books,
an Hachette UK company.
www.hachettelivre.co.uk

Picture Acknowledgements:
The author and publisher would like to thank
the following agencies for allowing these
pictures to be reproduced: Advertising
Archives: 44; Mike Agliolo/Corbis: 8;
Bettmann/Corbis: 13, 27, 28; Fabio Cardoso/
Corbis: 21; Thomas Cockrem/Alamy: 32; Kevin
Dodge/Corbis: Titlepage, 6, 24, 26, 31; EPF/
Alamy: 38; *Arthur Estabrook Papers*. M.E.
Grenander Department of Special Collections &
Archives, University at Albany Libraries: 5; David
Hoffman Photo Library/Alamy: 39; imagebroker/
Alamy: COVER, 17; Rajesh Jantilal/epa/Corbis:
22; KPA/Zuma/Rex Features: 30; Tony Larkin/Rex
Features: 45; Alain Le Garsmuer/Corbis: 41; Ian
Miles – Flashpoint Pictures/Alamy: 16;
Photofusion Picture Library/Alamy: 7; Jack
Picone/Alamy: 36; Christopher Pillitz/Getty
Images: 42; Jonathan Player/Rex Features: 15;
Reuters/Corbis: 20; Bob Sacha/Corbis: 9;
Science Museum, London: 10, 11; Sipa Press/
Rex Features: 34; Dieter Telemans/Panos
Pictures: 29; Time & Life Pictures/Getty Images:
23; Abbie Trayler-Smith/Panos Pictures: 35; Judy
Unger/Alamy: 19; Every attempt has been made
to clear copyright. Should there be any
inadvertent omission please apply to the
publisher for rectification.

About the consultant: Dr Patricia Macnair is a
hospital physician working in a small
rehabilitation hospital with elderly patients who
are recovering from major illness. She has a
Masters degree in Medical Ethics and Medical
Law, and has a particular interest in vulnerable
patients, end-of-life issues, palliative care, pain
control, obesity and weight loss.

Note: The website addresses (URLs) included in
this book were valid at the time of going to
press. However, because of the nature of the
Internet, it is possible that some addresses may
have changed, or sites may have changed or
closed down since publication. While the
author and publishers regret any inconvenience
this may cause the readers, no responsibility for
any such changes can be accepted by either the
authors or the publishers.

contents

Real-life case study

This case study highlights some of the issues that surround the debate on birth control.

case study

Buck v Bell

On 19 October 1927, Carrie Buck was sterilized under a new law created by the US state of Virginia. This law allowed people living in institutions to be forcibly sterilized on the grounds of 'feeblemindedness' or idiocy. The state of Virginia took Carrie's case to the United States' Supreme Court (USSC), and in 1927 the USSC approved the decision to sterilize her.

As a child, Carrie was taken to live with foster parents when her mother was judged to be immoral and incapable and was sent to a state institution known as the Virginia Colony for Epileptics and Feeble Minded. When Carrie was 17 she became pregnant and she, too, was sent to the Colony. A few months later her daughter Vivian was born and Carrie was deemed incapable of looking after her. Vivian was adopted by the foster parents who had cared for Carrie. At this point the officials who ran the Colony decided that Carrie was a suitable case for enforced sterilization. They claimed that Vivian was also 'feeble minded', and that her 'idiocy' was inherited. Therefore, Carrie should be stopped from having further 'feeble-minded' children.

This case, known as *Buck v Bell*, is now famous as the test case that led to a surge in enforced sterilization throughout the United States. Following the USSC's decision in 1927, more than 30 other states introduced similar laws. The reasoning behind such laws was based on the development of a new movement called eugenics. Followers of eugenics believed that human characteristics such as intelligence, physical strength and ability, and moral behaviour were inherited rather than learned or developed. They believed that people who had these characteristics were superior to those who did not have them, and that these superior beings should be encouraged to have children in order to improve the quality of the human race. At the same time, inferior beings should be discouraged or prevented from having children as they would weaken it.

Eugenics was particularly popular in the United States in the early 1900s. People believed that the country had a duty to protect and improve the nation's gene pool through the use of mass birth-control programmes, such as the enforced sterilization of those in prisons and mental institutions. To do this the movement needed laws to uphold such programmes. The USSC's approval in the case of Carrie Buck gave them the support they needed.

During the 1930s, eugenics was adopted by the Nazi government and put into practice in ways that few could have foreseen. As a result, the movement became discredited throughout the world. However, elements of it continue to reappear, especially in connection with developments in genetic engineering, and with various governments' attempts to control population growth.

Carrie Buck poses with her mother, Emma, in the grounds of the Virginia Colony institution. Accused of idiocy and feeblemindedness, the real problem lay in their being poor, unmarried and uneducated.

viewpoints

'It is better for all the world, if instead of waiting to execute degenerate offspring for crime or to let them starve for their imbecility, society can prevent those who are manifestly unfit from continuing their kind.'
Supreme Court Justice, Oliver Wendell Holmes, Jr. in *Buck v Bell*, 1927

'...the eugenics movement was a shameful effort in which state government never should have been involved. We must remember the Commonwealth [of Virginia]'s past mistakes in order to prevent them from recurring.'
Statement from Mark R Warner, Governor of the Commonwealth of Virginia, on the 75th anniversary of the *Buck v Bell* decision, on 2 May, 2002

It's a fact

In the 1900s, as many as 60,000 people were forcibly sterilized in the United States. They included people with mental or physical disabilities, people in prisons, Native Americans and Afro-Americans. Often sterilizations were carried out without people's knowledge while they were in hospital for other treatments.

CHAPTER 1

What is birth control?

When people use the phrase birth control, they usually mean the deliberate or artificial methods used to limit or to avoid having children. Birth control is also sometimes called family planning. However, this is a broader term and although it may include birth control it is usually taken to mean the whole process by which a couple actively plan the number of children they want to have and when they want to have them.

Limited by nature

There are natural controls on the number of children a woman can have. Women can become pregnant only after puberty and before menopause, roughly between the ages of 12 and 50. During this time, they are fertile (able to conceive) only for a few days in every month, depending on their menstrual or period cycle. Usually, women are not able to conceive (become pregnant) again if they are already pregnant

▼ In most economically developed countries, the majority of families have one or two children. However, some people still choose to have large families.

or for some weeks after the birth of a child – as long as they are breastfeeding and their period has not returned. Even so, in theory, a woman could have as many as 30 to 50 pregnancies during her lifetime.

Of course, this does not mean that all of those pregnancies would necessarily end in the birth of a child. As many as one in five pregnancies can fail in the early stages of development and come to an end naturally as a miscarriage. Also, there are some women and men who, for a variety of reasons, have difficulty in making a child or who are naturally infertile – unable to have children.

So why use birth control?

As there are natural limits on the number of children a woman can have, you might wonder why people use artificial methods of birth control, and it is true that many people do not use them. However, there are various reasons why people might want to avoid or put off having children at certain times in their life, or because of particular circumstances. For example, and in no particular order:

- they might not have a partner or a family to help them raise a child;
- they may not have enough food or money to support a child;
- they may already have as many children as they want or can afford;
- they may want to have sex without worrying about getting pregnant or having a child;
- they may not feel emotionally mature enough to have a child;
- they may want to delay having children for career reasons;
- they may want to avoid pregnancy because it would endanger their health, or to avoid passing on an inheritable disease, or disability.

▲ Teenagers are particularly at risk from unplanned pregnancies. In the United Kingdom (UK) in 2001, for example, nearly 8,000 girls under the age of 16 became pregnant. The United States has the highest rate of teenage pregnancy of any developed country, about 750,000 teenage pregnancies a year.

It's a fact

Having children is expensive. Research carried out in the UK by an insurance and finance company called LV (Liverpool Victoria) found that the average cost of raising a child from birth to 21, can come to as much as US$372,000 (£186,000), depending on where you live. This includes the cost of nursery fees and after-school clubs for working parents, as well as food, clothing, holidays, toys, and sending the child to university.

How does birth control work?

There are various types of birth control in use today, but they all fall into one of two main categories. Those in the first group are intended to prevent conception. This is the point at which a male sperm cell fertilizes, or joins up with, a female egg cell and a baby starts to develop. These methods of birth control come under the general heading of contraception, which means 'against conception'. Contraception can include everything from abstinence (deliberately choosing not to have sexual intercourse) to sterilization.

The second category is used after conception has happened. This is when the fertilized egg moves along the Fallopian tubes and attaches itself to the wall of the woman's womb. It can take about five days for a fertilized egg to fix itself to the womb. Once it has, the egg is known as an embryo, then after eight weeks it is called a foetus. Usually the birth control method used here involves some form of abortion (or termination) to remove the developing baby from the mother's womb.

If abortion is not used, people sometimes resort to infanticide – deliberately killing a newborn child. This practice is now illegal almost everywhere in the world although it does still happen occasionally.

Divided views

The difference between these two categories is especially important when it comes to considering the various arguments for and against the use of birth control, as some people feel that there is a strong moral divide between preventing the possibility of conception happening, and preventing the development and eventual birth of a child once conception has taken place.

Most people's attitudes to birth control are formed by their beliefs or religious views, the views of the society in which they live, their own experiences, or their particular social or economic circumstances. Arguments for and against using birth control often overlap, and a person's opinion may vary depending on the method used or the circumstances in which it might be used. Some people are

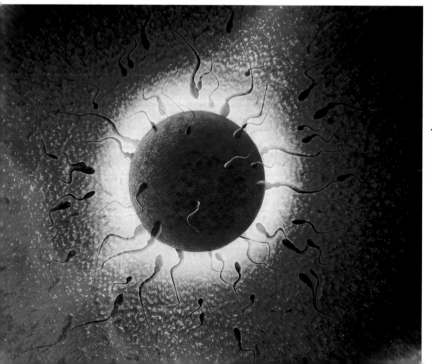

◄ Male sperm cells cluster around a female egg cell, trying to enter. Only one sperm can enter an egg cell, however, and the instant it does, the two cells combine and start dividing to create the complex ball of cells that is the beginning of a human life.

▲ As the world's population continues to grow, controversy about how big a part governments should play in controlling their country's birth rate is bound to increase, along with fears about how such controls could be misused.

wholeheartedly against birth control in any form and under any circumstances, while others feel it should be left entirely to each individual to choose for themselves whether or not to use birth control and in what way. Most people have a view that falls somewhere in between these two extremes.

A wider view

Alongside each individual's view there is also a wider argument, which has to do with the health and welfare of a society, especially in terms of women's health and the welfare of children. There are also issues concerning the ever-increasing growth in world population and the effects that this has on world resources, such as water, the environment and poverty.

Most countries in the world now support some sort of nationwide family-planning programme. Usually these programmes are voluntary, but a few countries operate stricter controls over the number of children their citizens can have, or the type of birth control that is available to them.

viewpoints

'You must strive to multiply bread so that it suffices for the tables of mankind, and not rather favour an artificial control of birth... in order to diminish the number of guests at the banquet of life.'
Pope Paul VI, to the United Nations Assembly, 4 October 1965

'We are given two choices – famine, pestilence and war on the one hand, birth control on the other. Most of us choose birth control.'
Aldous Huxley, *Brave New World Revisited*

▲ Sponges have been used as a vaginal barrier, either on their own or soaked in a paste or liquid, since the Middle Ages and are still in use today. This collection dates from the early 1900s and shows a mix of natural and synthetic sponges.

In the past

Birth control has become a big issue only in the past hundred years or so. Before this, lack of medical knowledge ensured that apart from abstinence, there were no really safe or reliable ways of preventing pregnancy. Also, for most people, life was a riskier business than it is today. It was common for mothers or their babies to die in childbirth, and many children who were born successfully did not survive to become adults. Having lots of children was the only way of making sure that at least some of them grew up to work and help provide for their parents or other family members in later years. Nevertheless, there were still times when people tried to avoid getting pregnant or having a child.

Even in ancient times, people understood the link between sexual intercourse and pregnancy. One of the earliest and most widely used forms of birth control was probably *coitus interruptus*, or the 'withdrawal method'. This is when a man removes his penis from inside a woman's vagina just before he ejaculates. Another method of birth control was to put various objects inside a woman's vagina to act as a barrier. More than 3,000 years ago, the Ancient Egyptians wrote out instructions for dipping a rolled-up wad of cotton into a paste made of dates, tree bark and honey and putting it inside the vagina.

Various herbs or potions made from mashed-up plant roots, parts of animals, and metal scrapings were taken to try to prevent pregnancy, or more often to bring about an abortion (a forced miscarriage) to end a pregnancy. Unfortunately, the ones that were most effective often contained poisons that killed or seriously harmed the women who took them. And, at different times in almost every part of the world, people have used infanticide as a form of birth control. Some used it as a way of controlling their population in times of famine or other difficulty, or to appease their gods. Or sometimes, it was used because it was less dangerous to the mother's health than trying to bring about an abortion. Today, infanticide is regarded as murder in most countries, yet even so, desperate people still occasionally kill their newborn babies.

Changing times

From the Middle Ages onwards, religious beliefs and views on the role of women as a wife and mother meant that birth control was generally frowned upon and not talked about in public. From the 1400s to the 1700s, in Europe in particular, midwives, and herbal 'wise women' could risk accusations of witchcraft if they dealt in such things. Much of the traditional knowledge of herbal methods of birth control was lost. In fact, by the 1800s,

It's a fact

Human life expectancy (the average number of years a person can expect to live) has improved dramatically in the last 100 years. For most of our history, the human lifespan has ranged between 20 and 30 years. In the first half of the 1900s, the average lifespan improved to between 30 and 45 years. Today, the world average is 65 years, although people in more economically developed countries have a life expectancy of 78 years or more.

many people, particularly unmarried women, knew little or nothing about sex or how people became pregnant. However, the 1800s also saw developments in science and technology that began to improve people's health, working conditions, housing and food supplies. People's life expectancy also improved, and more children survived to grow up and have children of their own. Population figures started to increase, and this gave rise to a new way of thinking.

◀ Male sheaths or condoms are thought to have been around for thousands of years, although the first written record of them is in the 1500s. Early versions were made of fine linen cloth, or of animal intestines like the one shown here.

A growing problem

In the early 1800s, an English economist called Thomas Malthus wrote several essays suggesting that uncontrolled population growth would eventually outstrip food supply and lead to famine. He proposed that people marry later in life and practise abstinence until they marry. Malthus's ideas influenced many others, including the English reformer Francis Place, who in 1822 began the first movement to publicly encourage the use of contraception, in the form of a vaginal sponge or cloth tampon.

In 1830, Robert Dale Owen published the first book on birth control in the United States. In his book he recommended the use of *coitus interruptus*. Meanwhile, advances were being made in other areas.

Condoms or 'penis protectors' made from animal skin or linen cloth had been used since early times, mostly in an attempt to protect men from catching syphilis, a sexually transmitted infection (STI). But in the 1800s, new technology made it possible to mass-produce more effective, lightweight, stretchy rubber condoms. In the 1860s, the *New York Times* carried the first advertisement for condoms. Rubber diaphragms and cervical caps for use by women as vaginal barriers also became available. Abortions, too, were on the increase, either by taking a wide variety of 'pills' and 'remedies', or by using the services of a private abortionist.

A new debate

However, not everyone was happy about this new attitude to birth control. Many wealthy traditionalists worried that these ideas encouraged a permissive attitude to sex, and undermined marriage and the role of women as wives and mothers.

In 1873, Anthony Comstock, head of the New York Society for the Suppression of Vice, persuaded the government to pass a law making it illegal in the United States to advertise or distribute 'obscene literature and articles of immoral use' – which included information about birth control and birth control products.

Over the next 40 years, Comstock himself used his 'Comstock Law' to prosecute thousands of people. Yet more and more reformers in the United States and in Europe began arguing for and writing about the need for birth control. For the first time, the subject of birth control and, by implication, people's sexual behaviour and the role of the family in society came into public debate.

Twentieth century pioneers

In 1916, Margaret Sanger, a dedicated campaigner for birth control, opened the first birth control clinic in the United States and was promptly put in prison for 30 days. Five years later, Marie Stopes opened the first clinic in the UK. Both of these women, their supporters and their clinics were fiercely criticized on moral and medical grounds, yet they began a movement that eventually led to a national network of family planning clinics in their own countries and elsewhere in the world.

The oral contraceptive pill was developed in the 1950s, and became available in the early 1960s. At first, it was offered only to married women, but within a decade it was also being used by unmarried women and teenage girls. 'The Pill' has probably done more than anything to change the role of women in society. For the first time in history, women had an easy and effective way of avoiding the possibility of childbirth – and millions of them chose it.

case study

Marie Stopes

Marie Stopes (1880–1958) studied science at university and became a Doctor of Science in 1906. A committed academic, she was also a firm believer in feminism and supported the battle to give women the vote. She married in 1911, but the marriage was annulled in 1914 after it became clear that her husband was impotent and unable to consummate the marriage.

In 1918, she published a book called *Married Love* in which she wrote about the physical and emotional aspects of sex between a husband and wife. The book caused a sensation. In Britain it was condemned by churches and other groups, and it was immediately banned in the United States. However, it was a huge public success. Thousands of women bought it and wrote to Stopes asking for advice – many of them were poor women with large families who were desperate to avoid having more children. Stopes quickly published a second book, this time a guide to contraception, called *Wise Parenthood*.

In spite of fierce criticism in the press and the threat of prison, Stopes opened the first family planning clinic in Britain, in Holloway in North London in 1921. The clinic was free, but provided advice and contraception only for married women. More clinics followed in other parts of the country, and in 1930 the National Birth Control Council was formed by Stopes and others. This later became the Family Planning Association. Today, the Marie Stopes International organization provides birth control information and services in 40 countries around the world.

▲ Although threatened with prosecution for writing 'obscene' publications, Marie Stopes was never taken to court. She remained an active campaigner on behalf of women throughout her life.

summary

▶ Birth control has always existed in some form or another. Supporters of birth control argue that using artificial methods is simply an extension of the biological limitations that exist naturally.

▶ There are natural limits to the number of children a woman can have. Critics of birth control say that artificial birth control is unnecessary and unnatural.

CHAPTER 2

Types of birth control in use today

The rights and wrongs of using birth control are not straightforward. Many people's opinions vary depending on the type of birth control in question, so it is worth looking more closely at the differences between the different types.

'Natural' methods

Depending on what people consider to be natural, in the main, these methods rely more on people changing their behaviour than on using devices or chemicals. As such, they have the benefits of having no side effects, are easily available and cost nothing. However, most of them are not particularly reliable. They include:

Abstinence – not having sex at all, or not having penetrative sex, which means indulging in some sexual activity but without the man actually putting his penis into the woman's vagina.

It's a fact

There are a great many myths about how you 'cannot get pregnant', including: you cannot get pregnant if you have sex standing up; you cannot get pregnant if you have a shower or bath, or wash your vagina straight afterwards (called douching); you cannot get pregnant the first time you have sex; you cannot get pregnant if you have sex while you are having a period. None of these are true.

It's a fact

About 85 per cent of sexually active women of child-bearing age will become pregnant within one year if they do not use any form of contraception.

Abstinence is the only natural method that is pretty much 100 per cent effective. However, there is a slight risk of pregnancy with non-penetrative sex if semen comes into contact with the vulva (the outer part of the female sex organs).

Coitus interruptus – pulling the penis out of the vagina before ejaculating sperm inside it. This is probably the earliest method of birth control and is still widely used around the world. However, it is often ineffective as it is extremely difficult for a man to judge precisely when to withdraw his penis.

Extended breastfeeding – also known as the lactational method. The connection between breastfeeding and infertility was understood to some extent by earlier societies, but its use was largely lost in the western world when the fashion for bottle feeding replaced breastfeeding.

Breastfeeding can be an effective form of birth control in the first six months after childbirth, as long as the mother's period does not return, and as long as her baby is fed entirely on breast milk. This means breastfeeding at regular intervals through the day and night, and always feeding the baby directly, rather than by pumping breast milk into a bottle.

Fertility awareness – this method requires women to work out the days on which they are most fertile each month so that they can avoid having intercourse on those days. There are various ways of doing this, but they all involve a certain amount of training and some very careful management.

Fertility awareness programmes are also used by women to find out when their most fertile days are in order to try to become pregnant.

case study

The Silver Ring Thing

In the United States, abstinence programmes are particularly heavily promoted by Christian-based organizations, such as the Silver Ring Thing. Using a combination of big live events with music, video shows, comedy and personal testimonies, coupled with smaller group study sessions, this organization aims to persuade teenagers to sign up to its abstinence programme. Those who do are then given the chance to buy a specially designed silver ring that they wear to show they have committed themselves to not having sex before marriage. If they have already had sex, the Silver Ring Thing gives them the opportunity to make a 'new beginning', and 'embrace a second virginity'. The organizers are not only concerned with keeping the youth of the United States virtuous, but they also say that abstinence is the only solution to halting the spread of STIs. However, there is growing concern in the United States that many young people who commit to abstinence may avoid having intercourse but indulge in other kinds of sexual activity, which increases the risk of contracting an STI because they do not use condoms as a barrier to infection.

◀ The silver ring is both a symbol and a reminder of the wearer's commitment to abstinence.

Barrier methods

All barrier methods use some sort of physical device to prevent sperm from entering a woman's vagina or womb, or from fertilizing an egg cell.

Condoms – the male condom is probably the most well-known and widely available barrier method, especially among young and unmarried people. If used correctly every time, male condoms are 98 per cent effective against pregnancy. But condoms are tricky. They can slip off during sex if they are not put on properly, or be torn by a fingernail or sharp object, or be weakened by age or by coming into contact with an oily lotion. However, aside from practising complete abstinence, condoms are also the only birth control method that is almost 100 per cent effective against infection from HIV/AIDS and other STIs.

Diaphragms, caps and contraceptive sponges – these are barrier methods that fit inside the vagina and prevent sperm from entering the womb. They are fitted by a doctor the first time to check the size is right, but after this the user puts them in and takes them out herself. They must be inserted before intercourse and left in

place for about eight hours before they can be taken out and cleaned. They have to be used with a spermicide cream, gel or pessary that contains a chemical that kills sperm. They are about 95 per cent effective.

Intrauterine devices – commonly known as IUDs, these are small, pieces of plastic and copper that are placed inside the womb by a doctor. They are long-lasting and can be left in the womb for a number of years. They must be removed by a doctor. IUDs seem to work by encouraging the womb to produce fluid that mixes with tiny amounts of copper from the IUD. This makes the fluid poisonous to sperm.

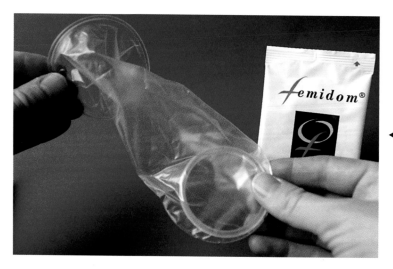

◀ Female condoms line the inside of the woman's vagina. When used properly they are almost as effective against pregnancy as the male condom (95 per cent), and equally as effective against STIs.

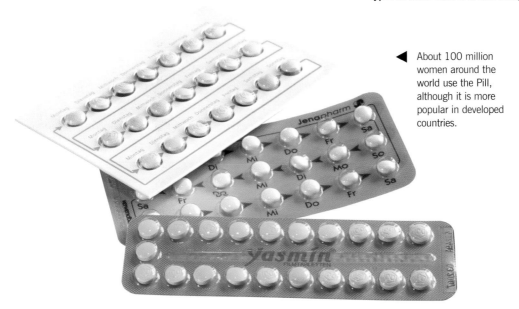

About 100 million women around the world use the Pill, although it is more popular in developed countries.

Another type of IUD, known as the IUS (intrauterine system), looks very similar to copper IUDs, but instead of containing copper, it works by slowly releasing the hormone progestogen, which works in the same way as other hormonal methods (see below). As well as stopping sperm from reaching the egg, both types can prevent a fertilized egg from attaching itself to the side of the womb. The IUD and the IUS are both 99 per cent effective.

Hormonal methods – these rely on women taking artificial versions of the female hormones oestrogen and progesterone. This 'tricks' the woman's body into behaving as if she is pregnant so that no further egg cells are released and conception cannot take place. The hormones also thicken the liquid at the neck of the womb, which makes it more difficult for sperm to pass through, and they change the lining of the womb so that if an egg is fertilized it cannot fix itself to the lining and passes out of the womb as it would during a normal period. Hormonal contraceptives are 99 per cent effective.

The first, and still the most widely used hormonal method is the oral contraceptive pill. There are two types of pill. The Combined Pill is taken every day for 21 days, followed by a break for seven days, and then another 21-day cycle is begun. The Progestogen-only Pill (POP) or Mini-Pill must be taken every day and at the same time each day.

It's a fact

According to the Office for National Statistics, 76 per cent of women under the age of 50 in the United Kingdom were using at least one method of contraception in 2006–07. Most used the Pill (27 per cent), then the male condom (22 per cent). Sterilization was the third most popular method: male partners (11 per cent) and the women themselves (9 per cent).

Other types of hormonal contraceptive methods include patches, injections, implants, and the 'morning-after' pill. The morning-after pill is also called emergency contraception as it is taken in just one dose, when a woman thinks her other contraception may not have worked or if she has had unprotected sex. IUDs can also sometimes be used as a form of emergency contraception.

Sterilization

Male and female sterilization is usually a permanent method of birth control and is used mostly by people who have decided that they will never want to have children, or who already have as many children as they wish to have. It works by blocking the two Fallopian tubes in women (these carry eggs from the ovaries to the womb), or by blocking the vas deferens in men (the tube that carries sperm from the testicles to the penis). In both cases, the tubes are either cut, sealed or clamped in a surgical operation.

Sterilization cannot usually be reversed if a person changes his or her mind. It is a very effective form of birth control, although very rarely the tubes naturally rejoin themselves and the man or woman can become fertile again.

It's a fact

A 2007 United Nations' survey among married women aged 15 to 49 found that female sterilization was used by 20 per cent of them, making it the most widely used contraceptive method in the world. It is common in Latin American countries, the Caribbean, Canada, China and India.

Abortion

Unlike other forms of birth control, abortion is used only after conception has taken place and a fertilized egg has begun to develop inside the mother's womb. It is normally carried out within weeks of a woman realizing she is pregnant. When a woman chooses to have an abortion it is called an induced abortion – miscarriage is sometimes referred to as a spontaneous abortion. When an abortion is carried out early in the pregnancy and under proper medical supervision, it is an effective and relatively safe procedure. However, because it involves removing, and therefore killing, a developing foetus, many people have very strong feelings about it and it is subject to massive debate all around the world.

Laws regarding induced abortion vary from country to country. In some countries abortion is either entirely illegal or may be allowed in extreme circumstances, for example where the mother's health is severely at risk or a pregnancy is due to rape or incest. In other countries, abortion is legal when carried out under specific conditions, which vary according to the

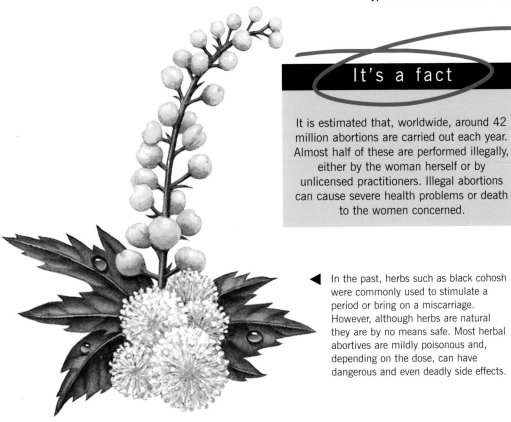

It's a fact

It is estimated that, worldwide, around 42 million abortions are carried out each year. Almost half of these are performed illegally, either by the woman herself or by unlicensed practitioners. Illegal abortions can cause severe health problems or death to the women concerned.

◀ In the past, herbs such as black cohosh were commonly used to stimulate a period or bring on a miscarriage. However, although herbs are natural they are by no means safe. Most herbal abortives are mildly poisonous and, depending on the dose, can have dangerous and even deadly side effects.

social, moral or religious views of the country. In countries where abortions are legal, they must usually be carried out within a certain number of weeks of the pregnancy, unless there is some overwhelming medical reason for doing it later. In the UK, for example, the limit is currently 24 weeks, although the majority of abortions in the UK (around 90 per cent) are carried out within the first 13 weeks of the pregnancy.

Legal abortions usually take place in a hospital or in a licensed clinic. There are various ways of carrying out an abortion, depending on the circumstances. Medical abortion involves the use of drugs to deliberately bring about a miscarriage. Surgical abortion is when some form of instrument is used to remove the foetus or embryo from the womb.

summary

▶ The only truly effective and least harmful form of birth control is to abstain from having sex unless a woman wants to become pregnant.

▶ Most 'natural' forms of birth control cannot be relied upon to prevent pregnancy or childbirth.

▶ Artificial methods of birth control, such as IUDs, the Pill, sterilization or condoms are far more efficient than natural methods and are therefore better at preventing unwanted pregnancies.

CHAPTER 3

Right or wrong?

For some people, birth control is a moral issue – is it a good thing or a bad thing, is it right to use birth control, or is it wrong?

Natural law

One of the more traditional reasons people give for opposing the use of birth control is that it is unnatural, or against natural law. Supporters of this argument say that sexual intercourse is a natural process that is necessary for reproduction, and if people did not reproduce, the human species would die out. Therefore, reproduction is a basic and vital part of human nature and an inherently good thing. As such, it is wrong to interfere with it, whatever the reason.

The alternative view is that human nature is neither inherently good or bad, it depends on the actions people take and the results of those actions. Humans interfere with natural processes in a great many ways, not least when doctors use their knowledge and skills to save someone's life. People are able to do this because they can learn and develop new abilities and this, too, is part of human nature. It is natural for people to use their knowledge and skills to adjust their environment and to adapt their behaviour to suit their changing needs. It is one of the things that has made humans so successful as a species – if they were not capable of change, they would eventually become extinct.

Behaving badly

Another argument given by those who disagree with birth control on moral grounds is that using birth control separates the act of sexual intercourse from the purpose of reproduction, and allows people to have sex simply for enjoyment. They believe that this is wrong because it encourages people to have sex

◄ The arrival of the Pill in the 1960s heralded a time of tremendous change in social attitudes towards sex. Reports published in the United States by researchers such as Alfred Kinsey, Masters and Johnson, and Shere Hite, shown here, exploded many myths and misconceptions about the sex lives of ordinary people.

▲ One argument used by Christians against the use of birth control is that by separating having sex from having children it undermines the traditional purpose and values of marriage.

outside marriage, weakens the role of the family and can lead to an increase in immoral behaviour.

Those who support the use of birth control argue that although it is true that removing the fear of pregnancy allows for greater freedom of choice over whether or not to have sex, this is not in itself a bad thing. They say there is nothing immoral about enjoying sex as long as it is carried out in a responsible way between two consenting adults. Similarly, they argue that there is nothing wrong with using birth control if the reason for it is a good one, in that it prevents an unwanted pregnancy. They believe that responsible use of birth control allows couples to strengthen the bonds of their relationship by enjoying sex with each other without the anxiety of conceiving. That this benefits families by allowing them to avoid having more children than they can support, which is good for the family group as a whole and means that every child in the family is a wanted child. Some people also argue that

if a couple knows that it is not ready to have children, it is irresponsible not to use birth control.

Others differentiate between types of birth control, and argue that the use of contraception is a good thing because it reduces the need for abortion which is morally less acceptable. However, opponents say that contraception encourages more people to have sex and does not always work effectively, so it leads to higher rates of abortion. In fact, according to research, the number of induced abortions has fallen worldwide between 1995 and 2003.

It's a fact

Worldwide, 63 per cent of women who are married or part of a couple currently use contraception, although figures vary from country to country, with some African countries showing levels of usage below 20 per cent.

Hinduism is the world's third largest religion. Hindus believe that people have a duty to get married and have children at some stage in their lives, but there are no specific teachings for or against birth control.

against God's purpose. Christian churches taught that people should have sex only when they were married and only when they were ready to commit to having children. During the 1900s, however, attitudes began to change. Many Christians now view sex itself as one of God's greatest gifts, with an important part to play in marriage aside from for purposes of reproduction. This has led to a divergence of views on the use of birth control among the different Christian churches.

Most Protestant churches are generally more willing to accept that there may be legitimate reasons why couples might wish to use birth control. In 1930, the Anglican Church was the first Christian church to issue a statement permitting the use of artificial methods of birth control as long as there were valid and moral reasons for doing so.

Other Protestant churches followed, and many now accept the use of birth control to some extent, while stressing that it should not be used to encourage promiscuous behaviour. Many Protestants believe that the use or non-use of birth control is a matter of individual conscience, although some still argue against any form of birth control on the grounds that it is against God's will.

Birth control and religion

The debate over the way in which birth control can affect people's moral and sexual behaviour often stems from a belief that traditional forms of marriage and family are the right ones, both for the individual and for society. It is a view that is largely supported by religious belief. Most of the world's major religions put some restrictions on sexual behaviour, and some specifically limit the use of birth control.

The Christian view

Until the 1900s, Christianity, the largest religion in the world, taught that the sole purpose of sex was for procreation, therefore it was wrong to use artificial methods of birth control as this went

The Roman Catholic Church, however, remains firmly opposed to artificial methods of birth control, both for the reasons given above and because birth control gives people the power to decide for themselves when a new life should begin, and they believe this is a power that only God should have. The Catholic Church does, however, permit the use of some natural forms of birth control, such as abstinence and fertility-awareness methods that allow couples to avoid having sex during a woman's most fertile period.

Islamic law

The second-largest world religion, Islam, also has differing views on the use of birth control. Islamic law forbids its followers to have sex outside marriage, but many of the various schools of Islamic law allow the use of contraception within marriage as long as it does not permanently prevent a couple from having children. So sterilization, for example, is not allowed. However, some Islamic teachers are completely opposed to all forms of birth control.

It's a fact

Neither the Bible nor the Qur'an say anything very specific about the use of birth control. Christian and Muslim rulings on this subject are based largely on interpretations of a few particular passages, such as:
In the Bible: 'Be fruitful and multiply.' (Genesis 1:28, 9:7)
In the Qur'an: 'You shall not kill your children for fear of want.' (17:31, 6:151)

case study

Humanae Vitae

By the mid-1960s, many Catholics were hoping that their Church would relax its view on the use of contraception, especially in light of the new contraceptive pill. Some bishops and priests were beginning to speak publicly in favour of contraception and the Pope at the time, Paul VI (below), ordered a study to be carried out. Rumour had it that a change was hopeful. But when the Pope announced his decision on the Pill in 1968, in the form of a document called *Humanae Vitae* (Of Human Life), he shocked Catholics around the world by reaffirming the Church's ban on all artificial methods of birth control. The Pope's decision was viewed by many to place an almost impossible strain on modern Catholics, and many do not, in fact, follow the Church's teaching on this point. According to a survey carried out in the UK in 2008 by the Catholic magazine *The Tablet*, half of the Catholics who took part in the survey used artificial contraceptives such as the Pill and condoms.

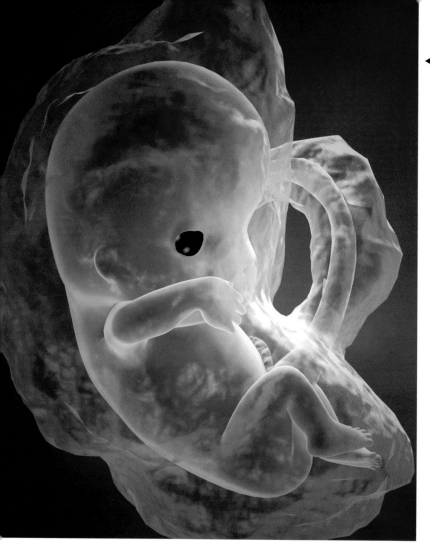

A key question in the debate on abortion is at what stage an embryo or foetus becomes a fully human individual. Beliefs range from the point of conception, to the point at which movement can be felt in the womb (16-17 weeks), or the point at which a foetus could possibly survive outside the womb (23-25 weeks), or birth.

Ending a life

The one birth control issue on which all religions agree is that abortion is morally wrong, although some religions accept that there are circumstances in which it may be performed. The religious view is that because abortion takes place after a life has begun and puts an end to that life, this is the same thing as killing someone. Killing is wrong and therefore, abortion is wrong, too.

Religions and individuals who hold the view that abortion is always wrong believe that a unique and separate human life (or the potential for a human life) begins as soon as a woman's egg cell is fertilized by a sperm cell. For this reason, some people also argue that using particular types of contraception is wrong because they can bring about a form of abortion, even if this is not their primary aim. By this they mean types of contraception such as IUDs, hormonal methods and emergency contraception, which can interfere with a fertilized egg or prevent a fertilized egg from attaching itself to the wall of the womb. This view is upheld by the Roman Catholic Church and to some extent by other Christian churches.

Other religions take a more moderate view and accept that, although morally wrong, there are some situations where abortion might be the lesser of two evils. For example, if a pregnancy puts the mother's life at risk, or if the foetus is so severely disabled it is unlikely to survive once it is born.

For those who hold that abortion is morally wrong but may be justified in some instances, the question then often hinges on how advanced the pregnancy is when the abortion or termination is carried out. For example, some schools of Islamic law allow abortion for special circumstances only during the first seven weeks of pregnancy, while others permit it up to the first 16 weeks of pregnancy. After this, abortion is permitted only if the mother's life is seriously at risk.

A personal choice

A more liberal view argues that the decision to abort or not to abort a pregnancy is a difficult and deeply personal choice and should be a matter of individual conscience according to the circumstances. However, most people who take a moral view on abortion believe that it should be carried out as early as possible.

Some people do not agree that abortion is always morally wrong. They argue that, in the early stages of its development at least, an embryo is simply a collection of human cells and not a person, therefore removing it is not the same thing as killing someone.

There are also people who do not think that abortion is a moral issue, although they may argue for or against it on the grounds of human rights or health and welfare. Others regard it simply as another method of birth control.

v i e w p o i n t s

'I am sure that deep down in your heart, you know that the unborn child is a human being loved by God, like you and me. How can anyone knowing that, deliberately destroy that life?'
Written in a statement by Mother Teresa to the United Nations' Cairo International Conference on Population and Development, 1994

'Morality becomes hypocrisy if it means accepting mothers' suffering or dying in connection with unwanted pregnancies and illegal abortions and unwanted children.'
Gro Harlem Brundtland, Prime Minister of Norway, speaking at the United Nations' Cairo Conference on Population and Development, 1994

s u m m a r y

▶ Many religions state that the purpose of sexual intercourse is to create a new life, which is a good thing and part of God's plan.

▶ According to some people, using birth control so as to have sex but deliberately avoid creating life is a bad thing. In particular, abortion is wrong as it destroys a life.

▶ Supporters of birth control argue that it is neither good nor bad, it depends on the circumstances in which it is used and whether the intention is basically a good one. They argue that responsible and thoughtful use of birth control is beneficial.

▶ For many people, abortion is not wholly wrong or wholly right. There are situations where abortion is morally justifiable.

CHAPTER 4

A human right

A great many people who are in favour of birth control do not see it as a moral issue but more as a question of human rights. These are the basic aspects of life that many people believe every human being is entitled to, such as the right to life and liberty, the right to freedom from torture or slavery, the right not to be imprisoned without a fair trial, the right not to be discriminated against, the right to own property, to work and to be educated, and the right to hold opinions and to express personal views without fear of punishment.

Reproductive rights

Supporters of birth control argue that every individual should have the right to decide for themselves whether or not they want to have children and when, and the freedom to select whichever method of birth control they feel is most suitable. Increasingly, people refer to this idea as 'reproductive rights'.

This view is supported by the United Nations. In 1968, the UN International Conference on Human Rights, which took place in Iran, included in its Proclamation for the first time the statement that: 'Parents have a basic human right to determine freely and responsibly the number and spacing of their children and a right to adequate education and information in this respect.'

▲ The United Nations also places particular emphasis on the rights of children. The UN Convention on the Rights of the Child includes the right to education and health care, and to grow up in an environment of happiness, love and understanding.

With regard to reproductive rights, the 1994 UN International Conference on Population and Development included the statement that: 'These rights rest on the recognition of the basic rights of all couples and individuals to decide freely and responsibly the number, spacing and timing of their children and to have the information and means to do so, and the right to attain the highest standard of sexual and reproductive health. It also includes the right to make decisions concerning reproduction free of discrimination, coercion and violence.'

case study

The Universal Declaration of Human Rights

The belief that there are basic rights and freedoms that all humans should have goes back to the beginning of civilization. Throughout history, different peoples and societies have tried to establish those rights and protect them by the creation of laws. In the UK, for example, in 1215, the Magna Carta was a first attempt to limit the rights of the English king in order to protect those of his subjects. Later documents, such as the United States Declaration of Independence (1776), the French Declaration of the Rights of Man and of the Citizen (1789), and the Geneva Conventions (1864) were instrumental in setting out the human rights laws and beliefs that exist today. However, it was the terrible events of World War II that prompted the 58 countries who became the founding members of the United Nations, to come together in 1945 to establish a 'shared vision of a more equitable and just world'.

The result, in 1948, was the first Universal Declaration of Human Rights. A document that states: 'All human beings are born equal in dignity and rights' and that everyone is entitled to these rights 'without distinction of any kind such as race, colour, sex, language, religion… or other status'. Since then, the United Nations has worked to refine, reinforce and defend people's human rights – including sexual and reproductive rights – in every nation in the world.

◄ The United Nations Assembly in New York brings together representatives from almost every independent country in the world. Their overall purpose is to work towards world peace and the improvement of humanity.

The women who campaigned for the right to vote in the late 1800s and early 1900s began the fight for women's rights. Until then, women everywhere had almost no rights in the eyes of society or the law. They could not vote or hold positions of authority, received very little (if any) education, could do only low-paid domestic or physical work, and had little or no control over any property or money they owned.

Women's rights

The argument for reproductive rights is seen as a key element in the fight for women's rights. Supporters of women's rights say that as it is women who go through pregnancy and childbirth rather than men, and as it is generally women who then carry the major responsibility for caring for their children, they are the only people who have the right to decide whether or not to have a child. Therefore restricting a woman's right to make this choice or denying her access to the means to make this choice (in other words, her access to birth control) is a form of sexual, or gender, discrimination.

In addition to this, campaigners for women's rights argue that lack of access to birth control discriminates against women because it denies them the right to the same level of sexual freedom as men, including the right to enjoy sexual intercourse without fear of becoming pregnant. It also limits women's ability to work and be economically independent, thereby forcing them to be dependent on their partner, family, or the state.

The right to choose

Saying that women should have these rights is not the same thing as saying that they have to use them – it is the right to freely choose for themselves without fear or hindrance that is important. Women's rights campaigners believe that full access to birth control along with complete and unbiased information and advice about it, goes hand in hand with ensuring that all women have access to skilled health care, advice and support when they do decide to have children.

In support of their arguments, campaigners point to the many risks that women suffer to their physical and mental health as a result of unplanned or excessive pregnancies, including death, infirmity and STIs.

They also argue that inequality between the sexes is a major contributor to the high rate of violence and abuse of women around the world, which, aside from causing them mental and physical damage, can often lead to unwanted pregnancy. They believe that denying women the right to birth control helps to maintain sexual inequality.

▼ Full access to birth control is still very limited in some less developed countries. Three-quarters of women in some parts of Africa, for example, are not able to get contraception or family planning advice.

viewpoints

'Sensible and responsible women do not want to vote. The relative positions to be assumed by man and woman in the working out of our civilization were assigned long ago by a higher intelligence than ours.'
Grover Cleveland, twice president of the United States (1885–89, 1893–97), written in an article for *The Ladies Home Journal* in 1905

'Violence against women is both a consequence and a cause of gender inequality.'
Joy Phumaphi, Assistant Director-General, Family and Community Health, WHO Study on Women's Health and Domestic Violence against Women

It's a fact

According to the World Health Organization (WHO) and the Guttmacher Institute, more than half a million women die worldwide each year due to complications in pregnancy or childbirth – that is approximately 1,500 women every day. Almost 99 per cent of these deaths occur in the less developed countries.

▲ Many women are divided over the abortion issue. They may support women's rights in other areas yet feel that the rights of the unborn child should outweigh those of the mother.

The right to life

Opponents to birth control also argue on the basis of human rights, but in this case they are concerned about the human right to life – in particular, the rights of the unborn child. Mostly this argument focuses on the issue of abortion, although it is sometimes used to make a case against all forms of birth control on the grounds that using birth control denies potential human beings the chance of life.

The human right to life, and the right not to be arbitrarily deprived of life, is clearly stated in the Declaration of Human Rights (see page 27), and is upheld by the law in most countries in the world. However, as with the moral argument outlined in the previous chapter, the big debate here is at what point does a human life begin?

Does life begin at fertilization as many religious groups believe? Does it begin at some stage during the development of a foetus from a cluster of cells to a fully-formed baby? For example, many laws on abortion limit its use after the point at which a foetus could potentially survive outside the womb. Or does human life begin only at the moment of birth, when the baby becomes a separate and self-sustaining individual? Everyone agrees that once a child is born it has the same right to life as any other human being, but at present there is no generally accepted view on the rights of a foetus.

'Pro-choice' and 'Pro-life'

The two sides to this debate are most clearly represented by the so-called 'Pro-life' and 'Pro-choice' movements. Both of these movements work towards establishing their principles as law, but they do so from opposite ends of the spectrum. Both sides incorporate a wide range of differing beliefs.

Broadly speaking, the Pro-life movement opposes any acts that threaten the right to life, including issues such as the death penalty and euthanasia. But it is most active in the area of birth control. A great many Pro-lifers are Christians who believe in the sanctity of human life, particularly innocent human life in the form of an embryo or foetus. They argue that the foetus's right to life should, in the main, take precedence over a woman's right to control her own body. One of their aims is to remove or greatly limit laws that allow abortion.

The Pro-choice movement came into being largely as a reaction to Pro-life. Pro-choice is mainly concerned with women's rights, particularly a woman's right to control her own fertility and pregnancy, which includes the right to sex education, contraception, safe and legal abortion and fertility treatment. It also includes the right to be legally protected from enforced abortion or sterilization, whether by husband, family or by the state.

case study

Roe v. Wade

In the *Roe v. Wade* case in the United States, the US Supreme Court decided that a woman's right to an abortion was part of a person's fundamental right to privacy as stated in the US Constitution. The USSC ruled that every woman had the right to decide, with her doctor and without government interference, whether to have a child or to have an abortion, at least within the first three months of pregnancy. This was a landmark case, as until then most states prohibited abortion except where it was necessary to save the life of the mother. Anyone performing an abortion in those states could be found guilty of manslaughter or even murder. The *Roe v. Wade* decision is controversial, with opinions dividing along Pro-life and Pro-choice lines. An amendment known as 'The Human Life Amendment' has been put before the US Congress a number of times since then but, to date, every attempt has failed. If accepted, this amendment would reverse the *Roe v. Wade* ruling, and make abortion in the US illegal from the moment of conception.

◀ In countries where abortion is allowed, men do not usually have any legal rights over whether or not a pregnancy can be terminated. Some people argue that as the father is legally obliged to support the child once it is born, he should have an equal right to be involved in the decision. In the last 30 years, a number of men in the UK and the United States have taken their partners to court to try to stop them from having an abortion, but to date all such cases have failed.

Disability rights

Advances in medical science in the past 50 years have raised another issue involving human rights and birth control. Using a variety of scans and tests, doctors are now able to identify at a fairly early stage in a pregnancy not only the gender of the foetus, but also the presence of physical or mental disorders. The question then is whether, and to what extent, people should have the right to terminate a pregnancy on the grounds of potential or perceived disability.

Many laws on abortion make a greater allowance for termination in the case of disability than for other reasons. In the UK, for example, the Abortion Act states that abortions must take place within 24 weeks, unless there is 'a substantial risk that if the child were born it would suffer from such physical or mental abnormalities as to be seriously handicapped', in which case an abortion can be carried out at any time during the pregnancy. The Act does not specify what the abnormalities might be, but leaves the decision to the mother and her doctors.

Probably few people other than the most dedicated Pro-lifers would argue to prolong the development of a foetus that would be unlikely to survive childbirth, or whose quality of life would be severely impaired.

▼ In a few countries, such as India, there is a strong cultural bias in favour of having boy children. In some cases, when parents discover that the sex of a foetus is female they will terminate the pregnancy simply because the foetus is the wrong sex. Although this practice is illegal in India, there is still an unusually low proportion of girls born there in comparison to boys.

However, there are serious concerns that sometimes abortions on the basis of disability are not fully justified. Campaigners for disability rights argue that differences in the laws on abortion are discriminatory because they imply that disabled people's lives are of less value than other, able-bodied people's. They also say that foetuses with disabilities should be given the same protection as those with no disabilities.

Right of conscience

Medical practitioners, such as doctors, follow codes of conduct that state that a doctor's main concern should always be the welfare of his or her patient. Doctors have a duty to respect their patients' privacy, and to make sure patients have all the information they need in order to make an informed decision about their medical treatment. Doctors also have a duty to abide by their patients' decisions and choices, unless there is a strong medical reason not to do so.

However, doctors themselves also have rights, and if they have a strong religious or moral objection to a particular treatment, such as abortion, they may claim 'right of conscience' and refuse to carry out the procedure. They may also refuse to prescribe contraception, including the morning-after pill and other emergency contraception. However, doctors cannot refuse to give a patient advice about what her options are and they should always refer the patient to another doctor who will be able to help her. In recent years, some pharmacists in Europe and the United States who are opposed to abortion have also refused to supply emergency contraception to women on the grounds of right of conscience.

case study

Alison Thorpe

In 2007, a British mother, Alison Thorpe, asked the doctors in her local hospital to perform a hysterectomy on her daughter to remove her womb. Her daughter Katie, who was 15 at the time, has cerebral palsy and is severely physically and mentally disabled. Her mother felt that the operation would benefit Katie's life by sparing her the 'pain, discomfort and indignity' of having periods, which she would not understand and would not be able to cope with. After considering the case for some months, the hospital decided not to carry out the operation because it was not medically necessary. The case sparked a great deal of controversy, with opinion divided between support of Katie's mother in her wish to do what she felt was best for her child, and the perceived infringement of Katie's human rights.

summary

▶ Human rights campaigners, particularly Pro-choice supporters, believe that individuals have the right to decide for themselves if and when they want to have children, and to use whichever method of birth control is most appropriate to help them achieve their choice.

▶ Pro-life supporters argue that an unborn child has the same right to life as any other individual and deserves special protection because it is unable to defend itself.

CHAPTER 5

Health and welfare

Research by the Guttmacher Institute, a leading independent research and education institute in the United States, shows that more than one-third of the approximately 205 million pregnancies that happen worldwide each year are unintended. Unintended or unwanted pregnancies result in major health and social problems around the world, especially for the millions of neglected and abandoned children that such pregnancies produce.

Unwanted children

Supporters of birth control argue that, with a global population of over six billion, the world has more than enough people in it already, so there is no social need to produce children. In fact, many would go further and say that those who are not ready to have children, or do not want to have more for any reason, have a social responsibility to avoid becoming pregnant. Many countries, particularly less developed countries, are struggling to cope with the numbers of neglected, abandoned or orphaned children they already have.

Many people argue that providing free and effective birth control to any woman who wants it is the only realistic way to reduce the number of unwanted children in the world, and would allow an increased share of resources to be spent on tackling the problems of children who are made homeless through illness, war or natural disasters, such as earthquakes.

Their view is that while all children have a right to a loving, caring and protective environment, preferably within a stable family unit, this aim is unlikely to be achieved by denying people full access to birth control. They believe that it is discriminatory and unrealistic to expect people not to have sex because they are unwilling or unable to commit to a long-lasting relationship or marriage.

◀ More than one million children are held in prisons or detention centres around the world, many of them awaiting trial for minor offences. About 8.4 million children work in the worst forms of child labour, including prostitution.

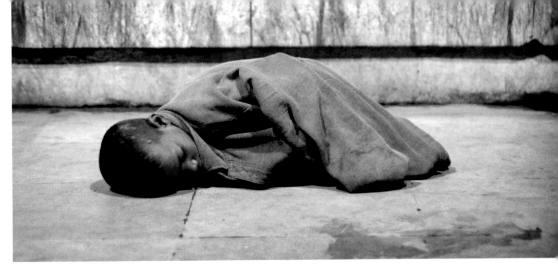

▲ Neglected and abandoned children exist everywhere in the world. The cause might be poverty, the breakdown of families, missing fathers, or underage mothers who are unable to cope.

They also argue that caring for children is time-consuming and expensive, and it is wrong to expect couples who cannot support the children they already have to continue to have more if they do not wish to do so. However, they also believe that it is wrong and unrealistic to expect couples not to have sexual intercourse just because they are poorer than other families.

Furthermore, supporters of birth control argue that girls and women who conceive children as a result of rape or sexual abuse should have the right to legally and safely terminate their pregnancy if they wish to do so. They say that it is discriminatory and unfair to expect a girl or woman to continue a pregnancy when she had no choice over the decision to have sex and had no chance to take steps to prevent a possible pregnancy.

The real issues

An alternative view to these arguments is to say that relying on birth control as a solution to these problems simply allows governments to avoid tackling the real issues, such as poverty and lack of education, behind so many abandoned children. Opponents to birth control say that more should be done to help poor families to feed and provide for all the children they have so that none have to be abandoned. They argue that with better education and work opportunities, parents would be able to take better care of themselves and their families.

Opponents to birth control also argue that more effort should be put into finding loving families to care for abandoned or orphaned children, and that governments and society should work to ensure that girls and women are properly protected from rape and abuse.

It's a fact

The World Health Organization (WHO) and the United Nations Children's Fund (UNICEF) have estimated that there are 100 million children living on the streets worldwide.

The Philippines has one of the fastest-growing birth rates and highest poverty rates in Asia. The government of this largely Catholic country does not allow national funds to be spent on contraception, although it does support natural family planning methods. It is not against the law to buy contraceptives in the Philippines, but few people can afford them, especially those who need them most.

Women's health

Another significant problem caused by unwanted pregnancies is the effect they have on women's physical and mental health. This is seen both in terms of the risks associated with pregnancy, childbirth and unsafe abortions, and also in cases where a woman or her partner may have an inheritable condition or disease that they do not wish to pass on to a child. Added to this, unintended childbirth can severely limit women's chances of improving their own lives and the lives of their families through education and work, and therefore trap them in poverty.

Without adequate and effective birth control, the only alternative to unwanted pregnancy for these women and their partners is to try to avoid having any kind of sexual relationship, which, say supporters, is both discriminatory and unrealistic. Yet many people around the world still lack accurate information and advice on family planning and birth control and do not have adequate access to contraception.

This problem is particularly serious in less economically developed or low-income countries, where, according to the research group Population Action International, 'unprotected sex is the second-greatest risk factor for health loss and the fifth-greatest risk factor for death'.

It's a fact

According to the United Nations Population Fund, it costs around US$7.1 billion (£3.55 billion) to provide present users in the developing world with contraceptive services. Each year, this money prevents:
- 187 million unintended pregnancies
- 60 million unplanned births
- 105 million induced abortions
- 22 million spontaneous abortions
- 2.7 million infant deaths
- 215,000 pregnancy-related deaths
- 685,000 children from losing their mothers as a result of maternal deaths.

Meeting a need

The reality is that many low-income countries lack the resources to provide free family-planning advice or birth control and rely on financial aid from more developed countries. This aid has decreased in recent years, especially from the United States. In January 2001, President George Bush reinstated an earlier foreign-aid policy known as the Mexico City Policy, which does not allow money to be sent overseas to organizations that carry out or provide advice or information on abortion. As a result, many health organizations and clinics in less developed countries have been forced to close. This puts many of the poorest and least-educated people in the world at the greatest risk as they cannot afford to buy contraception, even if they can find it and they understand what they need to use. This is particularly true for young girls and women who usually have no income of their own.

According to the UK's Department for International Development, illegal abortion is the only option for many women around the world when faced with an unwanted pregnancy. Illegal and unsafe abortions kill around 68,000 women each year, and cause serious health problems for millions more, including infertility and infection.

Making abortion legal and therefore safer in every country would reduce the risk of death and ill-health for women. For example, according to the Guttmacher Institute, after abortion was legalized in South Africa in 1996, the rate of infection resulting from abortions there decreased by 52 per cent. As well as making abortion safer, supporters also believe that making contraception available to all women would reduce the need for abortion.

case study

Illegal abortions in Latin America

Latin American countries have some of the most severe abortion laws in the world. Abortion is entirely outlawed in Chile, El Salvador and the Dominican Republic, and is allowed only in very limited circumstances in most other Latin American countries. Even in those countries where abortion is allowed there is very little access to it, and many doctors will either delay doing anything until it is too late, or flatly refuse to carry out an abortion. As a result, Latin America has one of the highest abortion rates in the world, almost all of them illegal. Some four million women have illegal abortions there every year and it is a major cause of maternal death. Also, as most Latin American countries are Catholic, access to other forms of birth control is limited.

viewpoints

'At least 200 million women want to use safe and effective family planning methods but are unable to do so because they lack access to information and services or the support of their husbands and communities.'
United Nations Population Fund

'It is my conviction that taxpayer funds should not be used to pay for abortions or advocate or actively promote abortion, either here or abroad.'
George W. Bush in a press release on 22 January 2001, on the reinstatement of the Mexico City Policy or 'global gag rule', which makes the receipt of US family-planning aid dependant on organizations agreeing not to provide abortions or information about abortions

Health risks

Those who argue against birth control say that although there are health risks involved in pregnancy and childbirth, there are also risks involved in the use of birth control. Aside from the dangers of abortion, some contraceptives can have side effects. In particular they point to the IUD and hormonal methods of birth control. IUDs, for example, can make women's periods heavier and more painful, and can cause vaginal irritations or infections. Very rarely, an IUD can puncture the wall of the womb.

Hormonal treatments, such as the Pill, can lead to an increased risk of blood clots or heart disease, especially in women who have a family history of these problems. There is also a slightly increased risk of breast cancer. On the other hand, the Pill actually reduces the risk of ovarian and womb cancer, it protects against pelvic infection and can make periods a lot lighter and less painful. In general,

the risks associated with pregnancy and childbirth far outweigh those associated with contraception.

Protecting against disease

A side issue to the debate on birth control, but an important one, concerns the use of condoms as protection against the spread of STIs, in particular HIV/AIDS. About 340 million people contract an STI each year – not including HIV – most of them women and many of them young. In addition, there are currently over 33 million people worldwide who have the HIV virus, with more than 2.5 million new cases every year. In 2007, 2.1 million people died from AIDS – 330,000 of them were children under the age of 15. The HIV/AIDS epidemic affects every country in the world.

There is no cure for AIDS, although there are drugs that can help to slow down the disease. Aside from complete sexual abstinence, condoms are the only effective

◀ Young people are particularly vulnerable to STIs. Worldwide, around half a million young people, especially young women, contract an STI every day (not including those who contract HIV).

means of preventing the spread of the HIV virus and other STIs via sexual contact. Delaying having sex, and having sex with as few partners as possible also helps. Those who are opposed to birth control argue that condoms are not always a reliable form of defence and that their use encourages people who have an STI to continue to have sex. Instead, more emphasis should be put on sexual abstinence as the only truly effective means to control the spread of HIV/AIDS and other STIs.

Interestingly, the Catholic Church allows use of the Pill purely for medical reasons to help women who have severe or irregular periods, but preaches against the use of condoms on medical grounds. They say that condoms do not protect the user against STIs. According to their research, the latex material used to make condoms has microscopic holes that allow the HIV virus, among others, to pass through. However, studies carried out by the World Health Organization (WHO) and UNAIDS show that when correctly produced, stored and used, male latex condoms are completely impermeable to infectious bacteria and viruses.

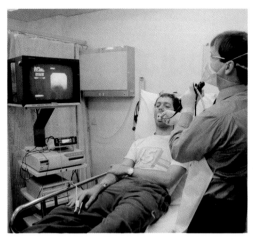

▲ Embarrassment and fear of social disgrace prevents many HIV sufferers from getting the medical help they need, even when that help is available. Ignorance and fear are major contributors to the spread of HIV/AIDS.

It's a fact

Many people in the countries where HIV is most widespread cannot afford condoms and rely on donations of free condoms from wealthier countries. In 2005, the United Nations estimated that at least 13 billion condoms were needed to help reduce the spread of HIV, while over 4 billion were needed for family planning. The total number of condoms donated that year came to just 1.8 billion.

summary

▶ Supporters of birth control believe that full and free access to birth control methods, along with accurate advice on how to use them, reduces the number of unwanted and neglected children in the world.

▶ Supporters say that birth control improves people's lives by reducing the ill-health and death caused by unplanned pregnancy and childbirth, illegal abortions, and STIs. This, in turn, helps families in their struggle against poverty.

▶ Opposers of birth control say that it offers governments an easy way out of tackling the real problems of homelessness, poverty and ill-health. They believe that more effort should be put into teaching people sexual restraint and in giving families the support they need to raise their children.

CHAPTER 6

Population and birth control

Currently, the world's population is 6.7 billion and growing. According to the United Nations Population Division, this figure is expected to reach 9.2 billion by 2050 – an increase of 2.5 billion people in less than 50 years. In 1950, the entire world population was just 2.5 billion people.

Many people are concerned that this level of population growth will eventually outstrip the world's resources. Although technology has improved people's ability to produce food, there is a limit to the amount of land and fresh water in the world that can be used to sustain human life. A growing population also uses more energy and produces more waste, further aggravating already chronic environmental problems.

Population growth varies in different parts of the world. A country's population is affected by its birth rate, death rate, and rates of emigration and immigration. In countries that have good levels of economic development, education and women's rights, birth rates have fallen and population growth has slowed almost to zero, although immigration to many of these countries tends to push the figures back up. In less economically developed countries, populations continue to grow rapidly in spite of high mortality rates due to poverty and diseases such as HIV/AIDS.

Limiting growth

Most people accept that an effective way of limiting population growth is to reduce the birth rate by means of birth control. In most developed countries today, birth control is widely available and is offered on a voluntary basis. In other words, individuals can decide for themselves whether or not to use birth control and when. However, at various times during the past century, a number of countries have tried to impose stricter controls on their population's birth rate, with varying degrees of success and in many cases in conflict with people's human rights.

For example, India is currently the second-most populated country in the world after China (see opposite). In the 1950s, India became the first country in the world to adopt a national family-planning programme, but although birth control information was made available it was not actively promoted. In the 1970s, India's government decided that drastic action was needed, especially amongst the country's poorest people who tended to have the largest families. From 1976 to 1977, a state of emergency was declared and thousands of men and women were pressurized or forced into being sterilized in order to meet government targets.

It's a fact

According to a 2007 report from a UK All Party Parliamentary Group on Population, Development and Reproductive Health, over the next two decades between 2.75 billion and 3.25 billion people will live in countries that face water shortages.

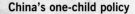

case study

China's one-child policy

China has more than 1.3 billion people and the largest population of any country in the world. Approximately one in five people in the world live there. China more than doubled its population in the last half of the 1900s, and in a desperate effort to bring its growth rate under control the Chinese government introduced a one-child policy in 1979. Originally intended to be a temporary measure, this policy forbids couples to have more than one child unless either parent was an only child themselves, or belongs to an ethnic minority. However, in many countryside areas of China, couples are often allowed two children. The most popular birth control methods in China are IUDs, sterilization and abortion. Policing of the policy varies from region to region. Couples that do have more than one child may be heavily fined. In some cases, government officials have forced women to have abortions, although there are regulations to prevent this. A side effect of the policy is that it has reinforced a traditional preference for sons, which has led to a disproportionate number of female foetuses being aborted and female babies abandoned or killed at birth. This has also created an imbalance in the population, which now has many more men than women. China's birth rate has slowed down, and the policy has led to many improvements in health care and work opportunities for women. However, critics of the policy argue that greater education and emphasis on voluntary reduction in family size would have had the same effect.

为四化一对夫妇只生一个孩

◀ A large poster on a wall in China promotes the benefits of a single-child family.

▲ The United Nations Population Fund has found that because of population growth, the number of people living in extreme poverty in sub-Saharan Africa grew from almost 231 million people in 1990, to 318 million in 2001.

Population control

Many people view the idea of government-run birth-control programmes with suspicion. They are concerned that such programmes might:

- interfere with people's right to make their own reproduction choices;
- create inequality by using financial rewards or fines to pressurize the poor or disadvantaged into using birth control while wealthy people do not have to use it;
- unbalance a society if too many people choose one gender over another (boys rather than girls, for example), or if they choose not to have children at all so that the population becomes an ageing one;
- allow wealthy countries to use family-planning aid to control poorer countries in an imperialist or racist way;
- be used as a form of eugenics aimed at removing 'less desirable' traits from a population.

These are all very real concerns. India is not the only country to have tried enforced sterilization. In the 1900s, the United States forcibly sterilized a great many people (see page 4) in the belief that it was necessary in order to prevent 'weaker' members of society from reproducing and passing on undesirable inheritable characteristics. Similar programmes were also carried out in other countries around the world, although most came to a halt during World War II. However, enforced sterilization was carried out on female workers in labour camps in the Soviet Union after the War, and in Czechoslovakia during the 1980s and 1990s.

Opponents of birth control point to the examples of China and India to reinforce their arguments against the use of family-planning programmes. In addition, many who are otherwise in favour of birth control are also made uneasy by the coercive nature of such programmes, on the grounds that they infringe people's human and reproductive rights.

Organizations that promote the use of birth control around the world believe that this fear is one reason why there has been a decline in recent years of the international aid promised by more developed countries to help meet the need for birth control in less developed countries.

At present, there are at least 125 to 200 million people in less developed countries who want to use contraception but are not able to. Supporters point out that most birth-control programmes in developing countries are voluntary and extremely popular, and that failing to provide family-planning programmes that meet the needs of the world's population not only condemns millions to poverty and suffering but equally infringes on their human and reproductive rights.

It's a fact

The United Nations estimates that between now and 2050, half the world's population increase will come from just eight countries. These are: India, Nigeria, Pakistan, the Democratic Republic of Congo, Ethiopia, the United States, Bangladesh and China.

viewpoints

'The [UN] Millennium Development Goals, particularly the eradication of extreme poverty and hunger, cannot be achieved if questions of population and reproductive health are not squarely addressed. And that means stronger efforts to promote women's rights, and greater investment in education and health, including reproductive health and family planning.'
Kofi Annan, Secretary-General of the United Nations (1997–2007), Bangkok, 2003, in an All Party Parliamentary Group report on Population, Development and Reproductive Health, 2007

'And now We wish to speak to rulers of nations… We beg of you, never allow the morals of your peoples to be undermined. The family is the primary unit in the state; do not tolerate any legislation which would introduce into the family those practices which are opposed to the natural law of God. For there are other ways by which a government can and should solve the population problem – that is to say by enacting laws which will assist families and by educating the people wisely so that the moral law and the freedom of the citizens are both safeguarded.'
Pope Paul VI's Encyclical Letter: *Humanae Vitae*, 25 July, 1968

summary

▶ The only way for governments to tackle the issues of global poverty, starvation and environmental disaster is to control the world's population growth by making birth control freely available to all who want it.

▶ Government involvement in controlling population growth all too easily opens the door to social, racial and sexual discrimination and abuse of human rights.

CHAPTER 7

The role of sex education

After a century of determined effort to develop and supply practical and effective methods of birth control, one thing has gradually become clear: one of the most powerful methods of birth control is education – not only education in its broadest sense, but also education in family planning, health, and sexual behaviour.

The education debate

Debate still rages over the rights and wrongs of sex education, particularly for young people. This debate mainly revolves around whether telling young people about sex and sexual behaviour encourages them to be sexually active themselves, or whether adults accept that most teenagers will naturally become sexually active at some point and need to be well informed in advance on how best to avoid harmful and potentially dangerous sexual behaviour.

Since sex education was first introduced into schools in the 1960s and 1970s, a number of studies have shown that comprehensive and consistent sex education can reduce teenage pregnancy and does not lead to greater than normal promiscuity. In the Netherlands, for example, schools use a carefully researched sex-education programme that pairs up the biology of reproduction with open discussion on contraception and the social values and attitudes that exist towards different types of sexual behaviour. The aim is to encourage 12 to 15 year-olds to talk freely about sex and to develop a thoughtful and responsible attitude towards making their own decisions about their sexual behaviour – and to give girls the confidence and skills to say 'no' to peer group pressure. This aim is backed up by government and media information

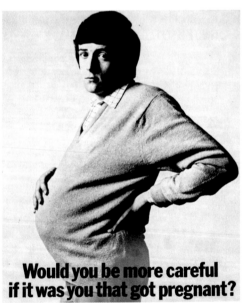

Would you be more careful if it was you that got pregnant?

It's a lot easier for a man to have a baby than for a woman. She's the one who has to hump it around for nine months. She's the one who has to grin and bear it. Backache, morning sickness and all.
It's not a lot of fun being pregnant, if you don't want the baby. It's not a lot of fun being an unwanted baby, either.

The Health Education Council

Anyone married or single, can get advice on contraception, from their local family planning clinic.

▶ National and regional public health campaigns to raise people's awareness of birth control began in the late 1960s and early 1970s. This poster, produced in the 1970s by the Family Planning Association of Victoria, Australia, became a symbol of changing attitudes to birth control.

campaigns, and fully supported by parents. As a result, the Netherlands has one of the lowest teenage birth rates in the world.

The UK, however, has the highest teenage birth rate in Europe, and the United States the highest teen birth rate of all the more economically developed countries (in fact it is only exceeded by developing countries in sub-Saharan Africa). One of the reasons for this, says supporters of sex education, is the lack of a clear, well-researched, consistent and wide-ranging programme for schools.

Although sex education is part of the national curriculum for 11 to 16 year-olds in the UK, its focus is on biological reproduction and the changes that take place during puberty. Any further teaching is up to the individual school, but open discussion is made difficult by the fact that teachers are expected to inform parents if their pupils admit to having sex or ask about contraception. Also, if parents wish, they can remove their children from these sex education lessons. In the United States, sex education varies from state to state, and ranges from comprehensive coverage of reproduction, sexual health and birth control, to abstinence-only education. About one-third of American schools teach abstinence-only sex education.

It seems certain in today's world that problems of a rising population, STIs, unintended pregnancy, poverty, health issues, and the ethics of abortion

are not going to go away. No matter who people are or where they live in the world, at some point in their lives they will be faced with a decision to make about birth control. Hopefully it will be a decision based on knowledge and choice – arrived at freely.

▲ Today, concern about the spread of STIs among young people adds to worries over teenage pregnancy.

It's a fact

As many as 14 million teenage girls become mothers every year.

summary

▶ Consistent and comprehensive sex education, taught in schools, is the best way to help young people make informed decisions for themselves and to avoid unintended pregnancies and STIs.

▶ It should be left to parents to decide what type of sex education to give their children and when. Too much sex education can encourage children to assume that permissive behaviour is morally acceptable.

Glossary

Conceive To become pregnant.

Conception The point at which a sperm cell fertilizes or merges with an egg cell to begin a new life.

Ejaculation The process by which sperm cells travel from a man's testicles through the vas deferens and then out of his body through his penis.

Fallopian tubes The tubes that lead from a woman's ovaries, where her egg cells are stored, to her womb. Conception usually takes place within the Fallopian tubes.

Fertile Naturally able to produce sperm or eggs capable of forming a new life.

Gene pool The range and diversity of genes that exist within a group or a population. Scientists now know that a large, very varied gene pool leads overall to a stronger, healthier population, whereas a selective, limited gene pool can weaken a population.

Genes Units of information contained in the body's cells. Genes are inherited from an individual's parents and describe his or her basic physical structure, development and behaviour.

HIV/AIDS An potentially deadly STI. HIV means Human Immunodeficiency Virus. Anyone catching this virus can develop an illness called AIDS.

Hormones A group of chemicals produced in the body that act on different parts of the body. Some hormones are also manufactured artificially for use in drugs, such as the contraceptive pill.

Menopause The point at which a woman's reproductive system naturally closes down so that she can no longer have children. The menopause is often a lengthy process and can take some years.

Menstrual cycle A woman's monthly cycle of changes in the ovaries and the lining of the uterus (endometrium). The cycle starts with maturation of an egg ready for fertilization. The egg is released to travel to the womb where, if it is not fertilized, the lining of the womb breaks down and is lost as a period or bleed, which completes the cycle.

Miscarriage The natural failure of a pregnancy when an early embryo or foetus stops developing and is expelled from the womb. Also known as a spontaneous abortion.

Oestrogen An important female sex hormone that regulates the menstrual cycle and stimulates the development of the womb.

Progestogen An artificial hormone, similar to the female sex hormone progesterone that helps to maintain pregnancy and prevents further egg cells being released while a woman is pregnant.

Sexually Transmitted Infections (STIs) A range of illnesses passed from one person to another through close sexual contact.

Spermicide A cream, gel or pessary that kills sperm.

Sterilization An operation to surgically remove or block part of the male or female sex organs in order to prevent the possibility of reproduction.

Vas deferens The tubes in the male sex organs that carry sperm from the testicles where they are produced, to the penis prior to ejaculation.

Womb (or uterus) The part of a female's body where a fertilized egg cell develops and grows into a baby until it is ready to be born.

Timeline

1550 BCE Ancient Egyptian records describe using vaginal barrier methods to prevent pregnancy.

1500s The first written description of the use of a linen condom is given by Gabriele Falloppio (who also gave his name to the Fallopian tubes).

1800s Thomas Malthus suggests that birth control, in the form of abstinence, be used to control population growth.

1838 Rubber vaginal caps are used in Germany.

1850s Rubber condoms become available.

1873 The Comstock Law is passed in the United States, making it illegal to advertise birth control, or distribute information about or devices for birth control.

1880s Rubber diaphragms are used in Germany.

1916 Margaret Sanger opens the first birth control clinic in the United States.

1921 Marie Stopes opens the first birth control clinic in the UK.

1930 In the UK, the Anglican Church allows the use of birth control by married couples. In 1931, the Federal Council of Churches in the US follow suit. The Roman Catholic Church issues a statement from Pope Pius XI banning the use of any form of artificial birth control.

1936 The Comstock Law is relaxed, although it is not struck down until 1965.

1950 India becomes the world's first country to adopt a national family-planning programme.

1960 The first oral contraceptive pill becomes available in the United States.

1960s The first plastic IUDs become available.

1967 The Abortion Act makes abortion legal in the UK up to 28 weeks. (In 1990, this is amended to 24 weeks.)

1970 The first reported cases of the possible side effects of the Pill are publicized.

1973 The United States Supreme Court rules that women have the right to have an abortion within the first three months of pregnancy.

1979 China introduces its one-child policy.

1980s onwards A range of hormonal birth-control methods become available, including emergency contraception.

1981 The first case of AIDS is reported.

2005 WHO reports that of the estimated 211 million pregnancies that occur each year, about 46 million end in induced abortion, of which approximately 40 per cent are unsafe abortions.

Further information

Books:

Sex, Puberty and All That Stuff
Jacqui Bailey (Franklin Watts 2005)

Reproduction (Understanding the Human Body) Carol Ballard (Wayland, 2009)

Websites:

www.bbc.co.uk/ethics/contraception
A collection of articles outlining the ethical issues surrounding contraception and abortion, as well as other topics.

www.brook.org.uk
A national, free and confidential sexual health advice organization specifically for young people under 25.

http://kidshealth.org/teen
The Teen section of kidshealth provides information about your body, sexual health, birth control and STIs.

Index

Numbers in **bold** refer to illustrations.

Ethical Debates

Contents of new titles in the series:

WAYLAND